GOAL
SCORERS

JONNY ZUCKER

Badger Publishing Limited
Oldmedow Road,
Hardwick Industrial Estate,
King's Lynn PE30 4JJ
Telephone: 01438 791037

www.badgerlearning.co.uk

2 4 6 8 10 9 7 5 3 1

Goal Scorers ISBN 978-1-85880-381-4 (second edition) 2013

Publisher: Susan Ross
Senior Editor: Danny Pearson
Designer: Fiona Grant

Photos: Cover image: Sports Bokeh / Alamy or Hugh Threlfall / Alamy
Page 5: Back Page Images / Rex Features
Page 7: The world of Sports SC / Rex Features
Page 8: Rex Features
Page 10: Mark Leech / Rex Features
Page 11: Offside / Rex Features
Page 13: Offside / Rex Features
Page 14: Neal Simpson/EMPICS Sport
Page 17: /AP/Press Association Images
Page 19: Gerry Cranham/Offside / Rex Features
Page 20: Offside / Rex Features
Page 21: Rex Features
Page 23: Back Page Images / Rex Features
Page 25: Andrew Couldridge / Rex Features
Page 27: Rex Features
Page 29: Neal Simpson/EMPICS Sport
Page 30: Action Press / Rex Features

Attempts to contact all copyright holders have been made.
If any omitted would care to contact Badger Learning, we will be
happy to make appropriate arrangements.

Contents

I. THE GOAL SCORER'S KIT

Whether you're a playground star or Lionel Messi, a goal scorer needs to wear standard football kit – a shirt, shorts, football socks and shin pads.

To score great goals, you must be wearing the right footwear. Comfort is the key. For playing on concrete or astro-turf, a lightweight trainer that feels good is right. For playing on grass, football boots are a must.

Many teams now ban metal studs because of the injuries they can cause. So it's worth checking out what your school or club says before you buy. Some boots have moulded studs. Others have studs that can be taken off, cleaned and put back.

2. PELÉ - THE LEGEND

For many football fans, Pelé is the greatest goal scorer in the history of the game. He was already playing in the 1958 World Cup finals for Brazil at the age of 17.

He scored goals from every angle and at every speed. He got tap-ins, amazing long shots and headers.

The most magical thing about Pelé was that he wasn't afraid to try out new tricks. Millions have tried to be as good as him, but no one has quite got there.

Pelé and Brazilian players with the World Cup 1970

3. THE 'HAND OF GOD'

In the 1986 World Cup quarter finals between England and Argentina, Diego Maradona's first goal was a truly 'remarkable' goal.

Maradona punches the ball past England keeper Peter Shilton

As the ball was crossed to him from the right, he jumped with England keeper Peter Shilton.

As Maradona leapt into the air, he punched the ball into the goal.

Shilton and the English defenders screamed at the referee and pointed to their hands to show that Maradona had used his arm.

The goal should never have been allowed, but the referee let it stand. After the game Maradona admitted it had been a hand-ball but claimed the goal had been scored by the 'hand of God'.

4. PENALTIES AND PENALTY SHOOT OUTS

A penalty is given if someone is tripped or pushed inside the penalty area or if the ball is handled in the box. It is then up to a player to take a 'spot kick' with only the goalkeeper to beat.

Frank Lampard is England's greatest-ever penalty taker

England v France, FIFA Women's Football World Cup quarter final

In some cup games, if the game is drawn after extra time then a penalty shoot out takes place. This normally involves each team taking five penalties. The team scoring most penalties wins the game.

If they are still even after this, then it becomes 'sudden death'. The first team to miss a penalty loses the match.

5. HOW TO SCORE

There are many ways to score a goal.

All goal scorers have different styles. Pelé was very fast and scored some great goals from a distance whereas ex-England and Newcastle striker Alan Shearer wasn't as quick but got lots of close range efforts and penalties.

Some are simple tap-ins where the scorer only has to be in the right place at the right time. Every good goal scorer gets some of these.

Some goals come from long range thundering shots. Bobby Charlton of Manchester United and England in the 1960s was very good at these.

Goals can come from volleys, half-volleys and headers.

Lots of goals are scored from free kicks.
If the ball has been handled then a 'direct'
free kick is given. This means a player can
score 'directly' from the free kick.

The world expert in scoring from direct
free kicks is Portugal's Cristiano Ronaldo.
His kicks swerve and spin so much that
often goalkeepers haven't got a clue
where the ball is going.

6. DIVING

Some players are so desperate to score goals that they will do anything to get the ball in the back of the net.

German player Jürgen Klinsmann is one of the most famous players to be called a 'diver'. This involved him running with the ball into the penalty area. When a defender came near him, Klinsmann would 'dive' to make it look like he was fouled, in order to win a penalty.

Some referees didn't buy into his tricks, but others were fooled. There are many other players who 'dive'. Some get away with it, but a number of referees give a yellow card if they think a player has dived. A few referees even show red cards for diving.

7. THE MOST GOALS

The player to score the most goals in their football career was Pelé.

Between 1956 and 1977 he played for the Brazilian side, Santos, the American soccer team, the New York Cosmos, and for his country, Brazil.

During that time he scored an incredible 1,281 goals.

The player who scored most goals in one match is Stephan Stanis. He did this in a 1942 war-time French cup game. Playing for Racing Club de Lens against Aubry-Asturies, Stanis scored an amazing 16 goals in that one game.

8. "THEY THINK IT'S ALL OVER..."

In the 1966 World Cup final, England played West Germany at Wembley. At 2-2, the game was incredibly tense.

England striker Hurst kicked the ball towards the goal. Hurst ran away to celebrate the goal. But did the ball fully cross the line? The referee checked with the linesman closest to the goal. He said the ball had done. The referee gave the goal. People still argue today if it really was a goal.

In the dying minutes of the game some people ran onto the pitch because they thought they'd heard the final whistle.

As they were running on, Hurst completed his hat-trick and bagged England's fourth. This led TV commentator Kenneth Wolstenholme to utter the famous words:

"They think it's all over...
It is now."

9. STRIKING PRACTICE

Here are some great tips to improve your goal scoring skills.

1. Stand in front of a goal and get a friend to fire corners in to you. As the ball reaches you, hit the ball at waist height into the net on the volley or the half-volley. Get your friend to take corners both from the left and the right.

Didier Drogba steps forward to take the last penalty in the 2012 Champions League final

2. Ask a mate to go in goal and practise taking penalties against them. Try to fool them as to which direction the ball is going. Use as many different penalty 'styles' as possible, e.g. straight along the ground or high into one of the corners. Try to score at least five out of every ten penalties.

3. Get two friends to stand either side of you. They take turns in throwing a ball high in the air towards you.

Your job is to jump and head the balls into the goal. Remember to use your forehead for maximum power.

4. Put five cones out in a line about two metres apart in front of a goal.

Practise dribbling with a ball round the cones and then as soon as you round the last one, shoot towards the goal.

To make this practice even better:

1) ask someone to be a defender behind the last cone to try to get the ball from you.

2) ask someone else to go in goal to try to stop your shots.

England Football Team training at Wembley Stadium

10. BECKHAM'S MAGIC

Playing for Manchester United against Wimbledon in 1996 was a young player called David Beckham.

He wasn't the world famous player back then that he later became.

Seeing Wimbledon keeper Neil Sullivan off his line, Beckham tried a shot from inside his own half. Only a great player would ever even think about trying a stunt like that. But Beckham pulled it off.

The ball floated more than half way across the pitch, above Sullivan's head and into the net.

Beckham had truly arrived! He later went on to become England captain in 2000.

II. THE BEST GOAL

In a BBC viewers poll, people voted a goal by Diego Maradona as the best of all time.

It was the second he scored in that famous 1986 Mexican World Cup quarter final against England in the boiling heat of a Mexican afternoon.

Picking up the ball from inside his own half, Maradona incredibly dribbled past the whole English defence and keeper Peter Shilton, before tapping the ball home.

You can watch this goal many times. It always looks truly stunning.

...AND THE FASTEST?

A few players have scored a goal in six seconds or under in a match.

In each case, the referee had only just blown his whistle for the kick-off.

Here are a few:

• **Ricardo Olivera**
(for Rio Negro v Soriano in 1998)
Scored in 2.8 seconds

• **Damian Mori**
(for Adelaide City v Sydney United in 1995)
Scored in 3.69 seconds

• **Keith Smith**
(for Crystal Palace v Derby County in 1964)
Scored in 6 seconds

12. HAT-TRICK MAN

Every goal scorer dreams of netting a hat-trick, but Japanese player Masashi Nakayama is the only known player in the world to score four hat-tricks in a row.

He scored them for his J-League club Jubilo Iwata in April 1998. In those four hat-trick games he scored five, four, four and three goals.

13. THE TEN BEST GOAL SCORERS OF ALL TIME

People talk for years about great goals and great goal scorers.

Pelé congratulating Ronaldo after winning the 2002 World Cup

Everyone has a different idea about who are the greatest goal scorers.

Here's one possible list of the ten best goal scorers of all time:

1. Pelé – Brazil
2. Maradona – Argentina
3. Ronaldo – Portugal
4. Gary Lineker – England
5. Paolo Rossi – Italy
6. Michel Platini – France
7. Gerd Müller – Germany
8. Marco van Basten – Holland
9. Ferenc Puskás – Hungary
10. George Best – Northern Ireland

INDEX